Unexpected Feelings
Andrea Sharp

Unexpected Feelings

Andrea Sharp

Copyright © 2021 Andrea Sharp. All rights reserved.

This book or any portion thereof may not be reproduced or used in any manner whatsoever without the publisher or Andrea Sharp's express written permission except for the use of brief quotations in a book review.

Printed in the United States of America

First Printing, 2021

ISBN: 978-1-951883-53-9

Editor: G.E.M.

Designer: Relate, LLC

The Butterfly Typeface Publishing

PO Box 56193

Little Rock AR 72215

Dedication

Firstly, I dedicate this book to God. He is the author of this book first. I dedicate this book to my mother and father whom I love dearly and miss deeply. To my children and grandchildren, you all are such a blessing to me. Also, my family and friends who believed in me, thank you. To my loving husband, thank you for inspiring me to be the best at anything I put my mind to do

And we know that all things work together for good to them that love God, to them who are called according to his purpose.

(Roman 8:28)

And so I tell you, keep on asking, and you will receive what you ask for. Keep on seeking, and you will find. Keep on knocking, and the door will be opened to you. For everyone who asks, receives. Everyone who seeks, finds. And to everyone who knocks, the door will be opened.

(Luke 11:9-10)

I can do all things through Christ who strengthens me.

(Philippians 4:13)

I won't always be this way.
(Andrea Sharp)

Contents

Foreword	xv
Acknowledgments	xvii
Introduction	xix
Quiet	19
When You Thought	21
Mourning	23
If I Had One More Day	25
I Find Myself	27
When People Say	29
My Normal	31
Replay	33

Make Your Day Worth It 35

When I Hear Your Voice 37

Will It Ever End! 39

Selfish 41

Finding Myself 43

The Only Thing I Have Left 45

Heal This Land! 47

Life 49

New Beginnings 51

How Can You! 53

Why Should We Love 55

Final Delete 57

It Was Not Over It Was Hidden 59

Sunset 61

Dear God 63

2020 65

Believing in Yourself 67

People 69

The Way a Man Is Supposed to Love His Wife 71

We Are Warriors 73

Behind Your Smile 75

Sisterhood 77

Nothing Is Wrong With Me 79

Pass the Baton 81

Removing the Blockage 83

Who to Call? 85

Respect Yourself 87

Quicksand 89

Just Because 91

When They Grow Up 93

What Does a Book Have? 95

About the Author 99

A Place For Your Quiet Feelings 103

Foreword

Welcome to a tiny fraction of Andrea's journey. She was raised in a small town called Mullins, SC. She was the first of three siblings born to Robert and Carol Gray. She is a mother, a wife, a grandmother, and a devoted friend to many. She is spiritually fit and will flex in any situation when necessary. She uses her gifts for good to benefit everyone in her circle and a few fortunate ones outside her circle. God made sure that the most beautiful and fragile contents are protected by the hardest shell. Andrea is a butterfly who has survived many storms, heartaches, homelessness, abuse, trauma, and the loss of loved ones. She has even cheated death twice. She takes nothing for granted and appreciates every beat that her heart makes, the very air she breathes, and being clothed in a sane mind. Andrea wants to share her experience with the world, a world that can be devastating, cruel, and unfair. She kills the enemy with kindness over and over. She has lost so many battles but is determined to win the war.

Kenneth Sharp

Unexpected Feelings is made up of many inspiring messages written during the most joyous and most challenging times of Andrea Sharp's life. Her writings are a testament that God is the source we need in everything life brings. This book will inspire you to see the brighter side of life at all times.

Pastor Karina Ravizee-Broussard

House of Refuge Christian Ministries, Inc.

This book, Unexpected Feelings, reflects some of our everyday lives and struggles. This book is a testimony about how God truly equips the ones He calls. This book has been written to bless and minister to all God's children. God has positioned and postured our sister to take His Word and her skills to create something that will nurture us spiritually. She has always been creative, and God knew the perfect time to birth something new from His soldier in Christ.

D'andra Williamson

Acknowledgments

This book would not have been completed without the encouragement of so many people. With their encouragement, I was able to push past everything to get to this place. I want to thank my parents. God blessed me with Carol and Robert Gray because, without them, I would not be here. My loving husband, Kenneth Sharp, thank you for being there when I wanted to give up numerous times. The prayers and encouragement you provided let me know I can do anything. Thank you, D'andria Williamson, HRC Ministries, Cassandra Melvin, Bianco Holmon, and Dr. Sharon Flowers

Introduction

I hope this book will help people understand the unforeseen emotional state or reaction in their everyday life experiences. I lost my mother on September 14, 2019. It was devastating. I did not realize I had the gift of writing poetry until my mom passed away. Each day something new came to my heart unexpectedly, so I began to write what I felt. I wanted my poems to help people who had or would experience these feelings.

Quiet

When all the calls and the visits stop and people go to their perspective places, you are left with this thing we call quiet. It can be very deadly if you let it, but it has a purpose. You can hear the beautiful voice of our God and even the loved ones you've lost. Still, for this thing called quiet you have no other choice but to submit and trust it because it is going to be a part of you. You can't get rid of it no matter how hard you try. God has a plan in this thing we call silence. It's scary right now, but when you allow God to fill the void that suddenly became a part of you, it will become easy if you allow God to direct your steps. Though the silence may return, we have to learn that what used to be there is no longer there. We are left with this thing called quiet.

Andrea Sharp

Question:

When was it too quiet for you?

When You Thought

When you thought that a certain situation would play out the same way it had before, you went through it numerous times thinking it would have the same results. Still, as you heard what was told to you and presented before you, in your mind you think this might end up differently. In disbelief, you walk out with tears in your eyes, and your heart begins to race. Anxiety starts, so you go to what you know best, prayer. However, your prayer doesn't have any effect on what is going on. When you go back, you realize this situation has gotten worse, and it is no more… when you thought!

Andrea Sharp

Question:

Have you ever expected something to be the same, but it wasn't?

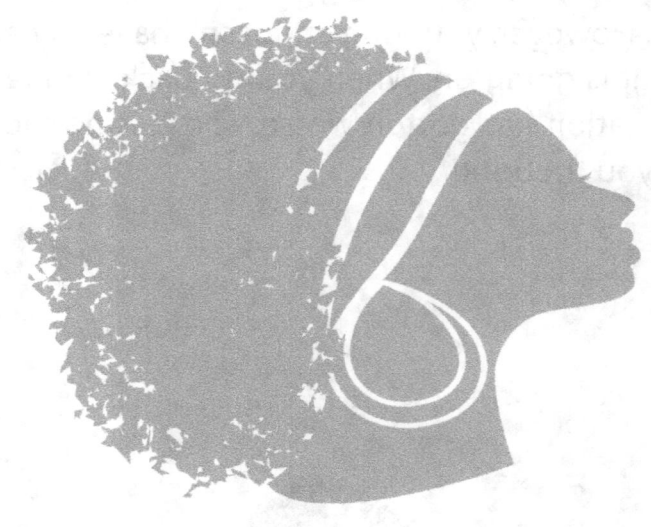

Mourning

Mourning doesn't have an expiration date. It only eases or doesn't hurt as much as it used to, but it's still there. It is a thing that is necessary to do because if you don't, it's going to affect your everyday life. It's has you walking around in a daze or a fog that you are trying to find your way through. Mourning will have your heart in pieces, but this is where God comes in to rebuild what has been torn down. It's a process that God allows us to go through either to wake something dormant in us or to mourn until we do not hurt as much when we think of the person we have lost. Mourning.

Andrea Sharp

Question:

How did you process mourning?

If I Had One More Day

If I had one more day, I would tell you I love you and talk to you for hours so I could memorize your voice and learn every inch of your face. I cannot say I would have done things differently, but I would have done things better. If I had one more day, I would give you kisses every chance I'd get. I would give you the things you love, but that one day is no more. So, I must live on the memories that we created while you were here...if I had one more day!

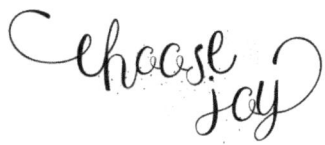

Andrea Sharp

Question:

How would you spend your last day with your loved one?

choose joy

I Find Myself

I find myself almost calling you to make sure you are ok or just to have a general conversation. I find myself trying to remember our last conversation, listening to the many voice messages you left, looking at my table where you used to sit, looking at all the things you gave me, and not getting rid of the things you left here. I find myself thinking of you almost every day, and when I realize that I did not think of you for at least an hour, I get upset because I do not ever want to forget you...I find myself.

Andrea Sharp

Question:

Have you ever missed someone?

When People Say

When people say, "Oh, call me, and I will be there no matter what," I know they have their own lives, but those words "I'm here" or "Call me anytime" stick with people who are going through loss, depression, or just need to vent. It is very important that you are sure you are going to be available because those people will remember and call you when they are going through hard times. Not saying that we have to talk to God first but God will put you in those people's spirits because you will have a word for them or you are there just to listen. So, just be careful when you say I'll be there...when people say!

Andrea Sharp

Question:

Have you ever experienced people saying that they would be there?

My Normal

My normal, I cannot seem to get back to it because you were a part of it. My everyday life, what is that anymore because there will always be a void? So, all I can do is try to do the things I did when you were here, but being normal is no longer here.

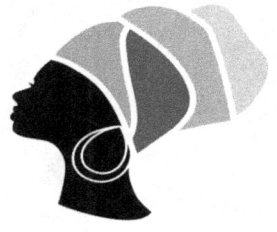

Andrea Sharp

Question:

What changed your normal?

Replay

I replay everything over and over in my mind. What you went through, I knew you were strong, but I did not realize how strong you were until you were gone. I had time to think about your life. I can replay all the things you told me. You felt embarrassed. You no longer have to feel that way. You thought you weren't beautiful. Your beauty was deeper than you realized. Though your mother no longer wanted you, now you are with your father who always wanted you. I replay our conversation about how excited you were to have a conversation with your biological mom. You met your brother and talked with your sister. God had all this in His plan so you can find peace in that area of life. The sickness that was causing you so much pain does not cause you pain anymore. You tried so hard to put the best on the outside by being who you were. You were a woman who loved to look good and loved being around your family! I replay everywhere you had been with me. I cannot fight these memories no matter how hard I try. They will always be on repeat in my mind, so I have no other choice but to put you on replay.

Andrea Sharp

Question:

What things replay over and over in your mind?

keep going

Make Your Day Worth It

What do you do with your gift? Hmmm...what do you mean gift? When God tells you to breathe and when He tells you to wake up, that's grace. Wow! Just close your eyes and picture God standing over you as He commands you to wakes up. So, make your day worth it because He has you here another day to work on your purpose, but wait, purpose is not something that you do not like. It is something that you have a passion for. You live and breathe this. So again, make your day worth it!

Andrea Sharp

Question:

What are the things that make your day?

Unexpected Feelings

When I Hear Your Voice

My heart cries out because it knows you are no longer here. It calls my name in that special way giving me the strength I need to get through my day and the encouragement to know I can do anything. All I want is just to answer it and say I hear you, Momma…when I hear your voice!

PEACE, BE STRONG NOW.
BE STRONG
DANIEL 10:19

Andrea Sharp

Question:

Is it someone's voice you wish you could hear again?

Will It Ever End!

The pain of this loss, trying to put the best on the outside, smiling when you want to cry…you don't want to be around people, but you don't want to be alone. Your bed becomes your sanctuary. You hear people say it gets better as time goes by. Then, you want to push the time quickly so that your pain can become a blast from the past. Will it ever end!

Andrea Sharp

Question:

Did you ask when a certain situation or feeling would ever end?

Selfish

Is it selfish to want you here so the pain can disappear? But you were the one going through the things that made you unhappy and always in pain. Is it selfish to want to tell you about my day or drive to see your physical appearance instead of an image on a picture? But all you want was to be free of all these thoughts and to be where God wants you to be. You answered His call, and now I feel alone. But is it selfish?

Andrea Sharp

Question:

When did you ever want to become selfish?

Finding Myself

Where am I now? Who am I? Finding myself is not easy when I look at qualities that look like me, feel out of place not knowing where to go next, and ask am I capable of my gifts. In Philippians 4:13 it says, "I can do all things through Christ who strengthens me." What are those things? Hearing people tell you what God says about you, feeling like you are pretending to do those things, trying to feel whole and at peace, and right now, it is an echo until I find myself.

Andrea Sharp

Question:

Where do you find yourself at times?

The Only Thing I Have Left

The only thing I have left is the memories we made together. The woman you've shown me how to become, how to treat people, and how humble you've always been, this mantle you left me is very heavy at times. I was told that since you are gone, who can they call but me. Sometimes I do not want anyone to call me. I want to be the one calling, but the only thing I have left is our memories.

Andrea Sharp

Question:

Name one or more things you only had left from someone.

Heal This Land!

I see all that is happening to the world. We all pray, "God heal this land," but God says, "My land is perfect. It is you that is not. I allowed this so you can heal your personal land. I allowed this so you can focus on what I was trying to show when things were normal, but you were not paying attention. Therefore, I had to shake up something and show you signs throughout the world. Still, you didn't believe I was God, so I had to allow this disease. Some still don't believe, but I will not remove it until I can heal this land and the land is you!

Andrea Sharp

Question:

What part of your land (body) do you want God to heal?

Life

I look around and I see life is giving, and life is taking during this pandemic. But overall, it is a blessing in all of this. No, I am not saying losing something or someone is a great thing, but it can be a life lesson. A baby born still has so much beauty in it, so the circle of life continues no matter what comes. God has a plan no matter how life happens. Just learn from whatever life brings you!

Andrea Sharp

Question:

What title would you give a movie about your life?

Relax
- and -
Recharge

New Beginnings

How can I embrace the new beginning without you picking up the phone for me to tell you the great thing that is taking place in my life? There is no one on the other end. How can I embrace this new beginning when I can't take you with me through it? I know your spirit is with me as I embrace what is new before me. My life's journey with you, I feel it ended so abruptly, but I am determined to enjoy my life because you would have wanted that. I know we have a Sovereign God. He does not make any mistakes. So, I will never give up on the point in time or space at which something starts.

Andrea Sharp

Question:

When did a new beginning start for you?

How Can You!

How can you tell a person who he or she is supposed to be or how to act? We must be mindful of how we approach an individual because the person might not be ready to receive what you are trying to deliver. How can you tell the person when to stop or how to get over a situation that makes him or her sad or even mad. Everyone handles every situation in his or her own way. How can you be the judge of anyone's walk in life or point the finger at the person? We must look in the mirror and see ourselves because we do not do everything perfectly. So, how can you!

Andrea Sharp

Question:

Have you ever been in a situation when someone approached you in the wrong way?

*Be love.
Be light.*

Why Should We Love

It's important to love. Love is like a seed to the soil. You keep showing all the affection that is needed for this seed to grow into the very thing that it was placed on this earth to be. Some don't know how to love, and some choose not to. Love is an intense feeling of deep affection. Jesus showed us how to love when He died on the cross for us. Still, we can't show love to someone by smiling and saying hello, or calling a loved one to say, "I just wanted you to know I love you today." I can go on with this because God wanted this for our lives. He made it part of the fruits of the spirit. He knew, as humans, it was going to be necessary for us to become the seed that was planted to blossom into what He created us to be. So, this is why we should love!

Andrea Sharp

Question:

What kind of love should we show others?

love grows here

Final Delete

We think that we deleted our thoughts when they no longer affect us, but when you smell or go to a place that reminds you of a bad experience in your life, thoughts start to come back, and you begin to recreate something you experienced. It's like when you have pictures that you deleted, but you can go back to the deleted photos and retrieve them. That's how our thoughts are. The devil will bring back things that you thought were gone. Thoughts will come to you like you can't do anything, or you are what people said you are. You know the "Read Easy" button that they advertise in the Staples commercial? Replace it with "Final Delete" instead. Thoughts will resurface, so we must hit the final delete!

Andrea Sharp

Question:

What did you totally delete from your life?

It Was Not Over It Was Hidden

I can remember my daddy's words when he said to me one day, "We are still slaves. We just getting paid now." I never understood what he meant until now. I understand what he was saying because of things happening in this world today. Our women are still being raped by the master because our men are being killed every day. They are trying to get rid of our men, so we cannot reproduce our race. God said in His Word, 1 John 3:16, "This is how we know what love is: Jesus Christ laid down his life for us. And we ought to lay down our lives for our brothers and sisters." I feel that instead of looking at the color of someone's skin, we must look beyond that because, in God's eyes, He does not see skin color. He only sees our hearts and character. So much hate clouds our judgment and allows the enemy to tell us what to do and what to say. It makes me sad, but I know God has a reason for all that He allows to give people purpose and to change things. What is going on right now will show us what needs to be done. 1 Peter 3:8 says, "Finally, all of you, have unity of mind, sympathy, brotherly love, a tender heart, and a humble mind." We need to work together and love one another despite how we look, but it was not over. It was hidden.

Andrea Sharp

Question:

Did you think that things were over, but they weren't?

Sunset

You may feel like the sun is setting on everything in your life but know it will rise again. I know you don't see it but believe that God is with you. Just keep that faith of a mustard seed. Even though I learned that suffering doesn't destroy faith, it refines it. I know that you believe God did not hear your cries, but keep looking to the hill because though we know that the sun sets, it will rise again. You will be made new!

Andrea Sharp

Question:

How symbolic is a sunset to you?

Dear God

Dear God,

Why does it hurt so badly when someone you love leaves and there is no more connection? Wanting to pick up the phone to say, "Guess what," or "I need to talk because I'm upset," or sad, I long just to hear the voice of him or her saying, "It's ok." I miss you giving me the best advice to get through this particular day. Dear God, why does death have to happen? It never heals. It becomes a hollow place in your life, and even your heart wants you to be filled. I know this [death] is something that I will have to participate in one day myself and know that my family and friends will feel what I feel every day too. I open my eyes because of the grace and mercy You granted to me. But God, why does it have to happen?

Andrea Sharp

Question:

If you could write to God, what would you say at this moment?

SHE HAS
FiRE iN
HER SOUL!

2020

Everyone came into 2020 saying, "This is going to be my year, and it is going to be different." I was one of the millions who said that phase. Oh yes, 2020 came in with a major impact. First, we got a virus that was invisible and took the lives of so many people. The coronavirus hit the world so hard that it turned our normal into our new normal. No, I am not saying that all of 2020 has been bad because God has uprooted so many great things in people who never thought this would be. On one hand, He uprooted some things in the world that needed to change like racism, specifically cops killing our Black people. God chose this year for a reason to let us know that He is God, and He is the only one who has the power of change. However, we must be willing to embrace it. Let us take a trip down memory lane as to what 2020 brought to open our eyes and change our land. What I mean by land is ourselves. The death toll of Covid-19 rises, the world's biggest lockdown begins, migrant crisis, locust attacks,

Andrea Sharp

Question:

How was your 2020? What would you change in 2020?

Believing in Yourself

In your mind, you fight with these demons in your head saying that you are not this you are not that. The enemy uses the voices of the people we love or even respect. It can even come from a post on social media. All these things can stop you from believing in yourself. Sometimes, it can be you allowing these words to keep bonded to you, and they play in your mind over and over again. It is going to keep happening until you scream the words,

"Would you shut up please! Stop! It's time for you to leave!"

If you don't get to that point, you will be haunted by what's in your mind for the rest of your life. So, now yell this with me. I'm well equipped! I'm more than a conqueror! I'm the head, not the tail! Keep saying these scriptures every time you feel doubt is about to come back. Now go believe in yourself!

Andrea Sharp

Question:

What does believing in yourself mean to you?

Strong
Fearless
Beautiful

People

Why do I get intimidated by people? They are human just like me. I feel like they are better, smarter, and well equipped you see. When I want to speak, my words get twisted, and my nerves get the best of me. Why is it that I ask they just people? I know, in my mind, that God made all of us different and unique, yet I'm intimidated by people. What makes me nervous in front of others is their reactions, but I ask God to deliver me, please. This is my pledge. I'm no longer afraid of men and their faces because, in Psalms 27:1, it says, "The Lord is my light and my salvation; whom shall I fear? The Lord is the stronghold of my life; of whom shall I be afraid?" Oh, did you hear that? As long as I have God, the fear has to disappear. God placed me here with a voice to tell his people about Him, so here and now, I'm no longer afraid of people. So, Devil, you can leave and take the people with you!

Andrea Sharp

Question:

Were you ever intimidated by people? Why?

Be you not them

The Way a Man Is Supposed to Love His Wife

I have seen so many men forget how to love their wives. They get bored so quickly and forget the vows they took when they stood before God. The way a man should love his wife is stated in Ephesians 5:25. "Husbands, love your wives, just as Christ loved the church and gave himself up for her." But I don't think they understand that verse because they don't know how to love themselves. So, they go out self-searching for something new still finding nothing but a void. However, men, I hope one day when you stand before God and your soon-to-be wife, you genuinely know what you're getting into because many years later, if you do not know God and do not know yourself, you will never know how to love your wife.

Andrea Sharp

Question:

How do you think a man is supposed to love his wife?

We Are Warriors

Every time we are on the battlefield fighting our everyday lives, we have put on the whole armor of God. Sometimes the enemy has us down, and he thinks he is winning. You must scream out scriptures like Isaiah 54:17. "'No weapon formed against you shall prosper, and every tongue which rises against you in judgment you shall condemn. This is the heritage of the servants of the LORD, and their righteousness is from Me,' says the LORD." Be like King David when he was on the battlefield fighting the Philistine giant called Goliath. He remembered that God was with him and he won that battle because he knew he was a warrior. So, remember who you are and know that, with God, we all are warriors.

Andrea Sharp

Question:

Whose warrior are you? Why?

Behind Your Smile

When a picture is taken, happiness tries to make an appearance. A smile in a picture has so many secrets and lies. Knowing behind each smile there is an illusion making everyone who looks at this picture think I am ok, and I am great. But really the smile has hidden emotions. Each emotion behind each smile may be experiencing disappointment, depression, insecurity, shame, confusion, regrets, and anger. So, do not be fooled by everyone's profile on Instagram or Facebook. Some of the smiles have some truth and most do not. Now, every time you look at someone's picture or even your own, you will wonder what is behind the person's smile.

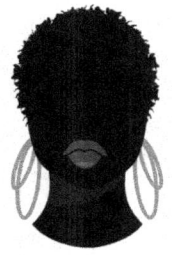

Andrea Sharp

Question:

What are you hiding behind your smile?

Sisterhood

Sisterhood means loving and acknowledging someone where she is at, giving the inspiration to build her up, helping her reach her highest potential, supporting her in becoming influential, and letting her know that God has a will for her life. Sisterhood qualities are important too. We have to demonstrate honesty, loyalty, and trustworthiness so we can help each other to make it through. What is important about having a strong sisterhood is the empowerment of women, understanding what you say matters, supporting one another, and knowing your sister has your back. It helps moving forward such an easy task. Let us build our sisterhood in such a way that nothing could take it away. Be happy for one another, be genuine and listen to what each sister has to say. Understand what I am trying to say. It does not take our bloodline to love each other the way God wants love to be displayed!

Andrea Sharp

Question:

What does sisterhood or brotherhood mean to you?

Nothing Is Wrong With Me

It took me allowing God to be a part of me so I could tell you there is nothing wrong with me. There is nothing wrong with me. My God made me beautiful you see. Understanding who I am and that I've been set free has made me realize that everything God made is made perfectly, so again there's nothing wrong with me.

Andrea Sharp

Question:

Did you ever feel like something is wrong with you? Why?

Pass the Baton

You are in the race, but you are not of the race. I am, so pass the baton to me so that your mind and soul can be free. I am the one who is running this race. Just let me be the one who will make you win first place. I am the champion of all champions that cannot be beaten. Reach your hand out and pass it to me. I am standing here to help you learn how to give your troubles to me. Now pass the Baton.

Andrea Sharp

Question:

When you are running the race of life to whom do you pass the baton?

Removing the Blockage

When a heart is blocked, there is an interference. The blockage must be removed so that it can have a steady flow and that the heart can work properly. The same applies to us. When we have a blockage in our hearts that is not letting us live our lives to their fullest potential or we are not letting true happiness flow like the blood that flows through our veins, we end up having a lack of understanding of what is going on due to the lack of oxygen. But like other things we ask God to deliver us from, ask Him to deliver you from this obstruction which makes movement or flow difficult or impossible so that you can live freely again.

Andrea Sharp

Question:

How do you remove something that causes a blockage in your life?

Unexpected Feelings

Who to Call?

When you do not know what to do or which way to go, who can you call when the people you value the most are no longer here? It's like you are talking to a wall. What I've learned is that God is always there giving you a chair. He is always giving you a listening ear. So, imagine you are sitting before Him telling Him all your fears and your desire. When all else fails God is always there. Remember, He is sourced to help you with your troubles when you don't know who to call.

Andrea Sharp

Question:

Who is on your speed dial when you need to talk?

Respect Yourself

I know he or she didn't respect you. It doesn't mean you have to disrespect yourself too. Continuing in a destructive journey, trying to do things you normally wouldn't do, has to be painful and has you in a place of apathy, but understand – you have to. Just because you feel that they destroyed your heart doesn't mean that you have to destroy it as well. Go back to your first love. You know just as well as I do, God is our Prince of Peace and He knows how to respect us, treat us, and teach us how to love and respect ourselves too.

Andrea Sharp

Question:

What are the ways you need to respect yourself? How do you get back to respecting yourself?

Quicksand

It is a loose wet sand that yields easily to pressure and sucks in anything resting on or falling into it. It is a representation of our lives. Do not allow it to pull you in. Every time you try to escape, it devours you. Here is the escape plan. Reach out to our Lord and Savior. He will save you. (Psalm 71:2) In Your righteousness deliver me and rescue me;

Incline Your ear to me and save me. Understand that He is God. Reach up and He will save you!

keep going

Andrea Sharp

Question:

Did life make you feel like you are being pulled under or like you are in quicksand?

keep going

Just Because

I love you just because. God told me that you are the one, and He told me why. We got married in a blink of an eye. People did not believe in our marriage just because of how fast our love grew. Despite what people thought, we made it through. God reminds me of your love each day through the things you do and things you say. I love you today. I love you tomorrow. I love you just because.

Andrea Sharp

Question:

What did you do just because?
Who did you do it for?

life is now

Unexpected Feelings

When They Grow Up

The day they are placed in your arms, you want to keep them safe from anything or anyone that may try to take them away. You feed and clothe them. You try to show them the way. You teach them how to love and respect and how to get through day to day. But, when the years pass by, they become who they are. Their need for you seems so very far. Your arms stretched wide, but you finally realized when they grow up, you become pint-sized.

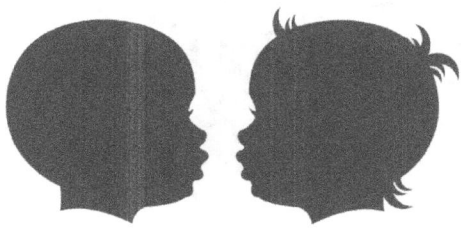

Andrea Sharp

Question:

How do you feel when your children grow up?

What Does a Book Have?

A beginning, a middle, and an end, I heard all the time that God is the Author and the Finisher.

God is like a book. He is your beginning, your middle, and your end. No matter what you are going through, God has control over your beginning, when we are born. He has control over your middle, when you are going through your everyday life, and your end, your purpose, and plan for your life until He calls you home back to dust. So, do not let your beginning and your middle dictate what your end is going to be. I know things look bad and your back is against the wall, but your purpose will not let you give up. Every time you get weak, the purpose that God placed in you keeps popping up, and you keep going and pushing towards your destiny. So, remember that God is like a book. He is your beginning, your middle, and your end!

Question:

If your life were a book what would you want it to illustrate?

About the Author

Unexpected Feelings is a book of poetry by first-time author Andrea Sharp. After the loss of her mother, the author began experiencing what she is calling Unexpected Feelings. These random and sometimes intrusive thoughts were so powerful, she was compelled to write them down. Later during her quiet time, she would read what she'd written and find solace. She prays that her poems will bring comfort to you as well.

Butterfly Typeface Publishing

Contact us for all your publishing & writing needs!

Iris M Williams

PO Box 56193

Little Rock AR 72215

www.butterflytypeface.com

A Place For Your Quiet Feelings

Grief is how we deal with loss and it is an individualistic process. No two people will grieve exactly the same. You should not compare the way you handle loss to the way someone else handles loss. Often you will not know what to expect until you are faced with the challenge so there really is not a way to prepare.

My advice is to seek the guidance of your Heavenly Father.

Releasing your feelings is also a good idea. These next few pages are provided for you to write whatever you are feeling about your loss. It could in the form of poetry, a story, doodles, or even random thoughts. The goal is to purge your heart and mind.

Do not be afraid of the feelings that will come when you get still and quiet.

Andrea Sharp

Relax
—and—
Recharge

Relax -and- Recharge

Relax
-and-
Recharge

Relax -and- Recharge

Relax
-and-
Recharge

Relax
-and-
Recharge

Relax
-and-
Recharge

Relax -and- Recharge

Relax
-and-
Recharge

Relax
-and-
Recharge

Relax
-and-
Recharge

Relax
-and-
Recharge

Relax
-and-
Recharge

Relax
-and-
Recharge

Relax
-and-
Recharge

Relax
-and-
Recharge

Relax
-and-
Recharge

Relax
-and-
Recharge

Relax
-and-
Recharge

Relax
-and-
Recharge

Relax
– and –
Recharge

Relax
-and-
Recharge

Relax -and- Recharge

Relax
-and-
Recharge

Relax
-and-
Recharge

Relax
-and-
Recharge

Relax
-and-
Recharge

Relax
-and-
Recharge

Relax
-and-
Recharge

Relax -and- Recharge

www.ingramcontent.com/pod-product-compliance
Lightning Source LLC
Chambersburg PA
CBHW072029110526
44592CB00012B/1437